DEFENDING HUMAN DIGNITY: THE ROLE OF
THE HUMAN RIGHTS ACTIVIST AND THE SCHOLAR

THEO VAN BOVEN LECTURES – MAASTRICHT UNIVERSITY
FONS COOMANS (editor)

Theo van Boven Lecture Series – Volume 3

DEFENDING HUMAN DIGNITY: THE ROLE OF THE HUMAN RIGHTS ACTIVIST AND THE SCHOLAR

Fons COOMANS (editor)

Cambridge – Antwerp – Portland

Intersentia Ltd
Sheraton House | Castle Park
Cambridge | CB3 0AX | United Kingdom
Tel.: +44 1223 370 170 | Fax: +44 1223 370 169
Email: mail@intersentia.co.uk
www.intersentia.com | www.intersentia.co.uk

Distribution for the UK and Ireland:
NBN International
Airport Business Centre, 10 Thornbury Road
Plymouth, PL6 7PP
United Kingdom
Tel: +44 1752 202 301 | Fax: +44 1752 202 331
Email: orders@nbninternational.com

Distribution for Europe and all other countries:
Intersentia Publishing nv
Groenstraat 31
2640 Mortsel
Belgium
Tel.: +32 3 680 15 50 | Fax: +32 3 658 71 21
Email: mail@intersentia.be

Distribution for the USA and Canada:
International Specialized Book Services
920 NE 58th Ave Suite 300
Portland, OR 97213
USA
Tel.: +1 800 944 6190 (toll free) | Fax: +1 503 280 8832
Email: info@isbs.com

Defending Human Dignity: the Role of the Human Rights Activist and the Scholar
© 2017 The editor and contributors severally

The author has asserted the right under the Copyright, Designs and Patents Act 1988, to be identified as author of this work.

No part of this book may be reproduced, stored in a retrieval system, or transmitted, in any form, or by any means, without prior written permission from Intersentia, or as expressly permitted by law or under the terms agreed with the appropriate reprographic rights organisation. Enquiries concerning reproduction which may not be covered by the above should be addressed to Intersentia at the address above.

ISBN 978-1-78068-444-4
D/2016/7849/171
NUR 828

British Library Cataloguing in Publication Data. A catalogue record for this book is available from the British Library.

Contents

5th Annual Theo van Boven Lecture   7

Defending Rights: Human Rights Defenders in the Front Line
Hina Jilani   9

6th Annual Theo van Boven Lecture   19

Slavery and the Human Rights Scholars
Jean Allain   21

The Politics of Human Rights: Slavery and the Sustainable Development Goals
Aidan McQuade   41

The present booklet contains the texts of the Theo van Boven Lectures held in 2014 and 2015. These annual lectures are organized by the Maastricht Centre for Human Rights in honour of Professor Theo van Boven, co-founder of the Centre.

5th Annual Theo van Boven Lecture

Maastricht University

12 November 2014

Introduction

On Wednesday 12 November 2014 the 5th Theo van Boven lecture was held at the Faculty of Law.

The 2014 lecture was delivered by Mrs. Hilani Jilani from Pakistan. The title of her address was "Defending Rights: Human Rights Defenders in the Front Line". Human rights defenders are persons, groups or organisations who stand up and speak out for respect and protection of human rights. They denounce human rights violations by states and non-state actors. In many cases human rights defenders have been subject to harassment, threats, arrest, detention, unfair trials, ill-treatment and sometimes killings.
Mrs. Jilani was the first Special Representative of the United Nations Secretary-General on Human Rights Defenders from 2000–2008. This position performs an important protective function where human rights of defenders are at risk.

Hina Jilani is internationally recognised for her expertise in critical human rights investigations. In February 1980 with her sister Asma Jahangir, she co-founded Pakistan's first all-female legal aid practice, AGHS Legal Aid Cell (ALAC) in Lahore. Initially the activities were confined to providing legal aid to women, but gradually these activities increased to including legal awareness, education, protection from exploitation, legal research, counselling and providing legal assistance as well. She is also one of the founders of the Human Rights Commission of Pakistan and the Women's Action Forum (WAF) (a pressure group established in 1980 campaigning against discriminatory legislation) and also founded Pakistan's first legal aid centre in 1986. A lawyer and civil society activist and active in the movement for peace, human rights and women's rights in Pakistan for the last three decades, she specialises in human rights litigation, and is especially concerned with the human rights of women, children, minorities, bonded and child labour, political and other prisoners. She has conducted several cases which have become landmarks in setting human rights standards in Pakistan. In July 2013, she joined The Elders, a group of statesmen, peace activists and human rights advocates, brought together by Nelson Mandela.[1]

---

1   Information retrieved from Wikipedia.

Defending Rights: Human Rights Defenders in the Front Line

Hina Jilani

Human rights defenders are fundamental actors in any effort to implement the overall international human rights framework. Establishing promoting and sustaining democracy, maintaining international peace and security and providing or advancing a people oriented agenda for development cannot be accomplished without the contributions that human rights defenders make. The role of human rights defenders has attained a critical significance in the light of armed conflicts, political tensions, economic disparities and the erosion of human rights standards that mark the current global climate. Establishing promoting and sustaining democracy, maintaining international peace and security and advancing a people's agenda for development cannot be accomplished without their contributions.

Defenders bring to the fore information on the realities of situations to be addressed without which national and international efforts would be ineffective and contribute to poverty alleviation, humanitarian assistance, and post-conflict reconstruction, and to improving individual indicators of development such as access to health care and adult literacy, among many other activities. In situations of crises, their presence is known to have calmed situations and, at times, to prevent human rights violations from being committed. While support for human rights and democracy in structures of the State is slow to emerge, or may even have suffered a reversal in some cases, civil society has demonstrated a strong resolve to resist authoritarianism and oppression. Human rights defenders and other civil society actors have played a significant role in bringing recognition of the concepts of participatory democracy, transparency and accountability by both the state and the society. They are in the frontline striving to establish facts and bringing these to public attention, protecting and assisting victims and demanding for justice. When internal systems become unresponsive, it is human rights defenders who call for support from the international community.

This was not easily done. While their work is indispensable for any national or international system for the protection and promotion of human rights, defenders have suffered harm and face grievous threats to their life, liberty, security, independence and credibility. State apparatus, oppressive laws and other tools of repression continue to be used against defenders in attempts to deter them from their valuable work in defence of rights. Human rights defenders all over the world are subjected to assassinations, disappearances, illegal arrest and detention, and torture. In several countries defenders have suffered arrest and detention, unfair trial and denial of due process after false cases were registered against them as a tactic of harassment.

Added to these are vilification campaigns and negative propaganda against human rights defenders. In many instances such propaganda is initiated by the intelligence agencies of the State and propagated by unscrupulous use of the media. Such propaganda often precedes acts of violence against defenders and the constituencies they represent. A number of human rights defenders are living in self-imposed exile after having to flee their country to safeguard their lives or liberty. Individuals and groups who have reported human rights abuse to international bodies, including the United Nations human rights mechanisms have suffered reprisals and other serious harm.

Human rights defenders have been targeted in their professional capacity as NGO workers, human rights lawyers, trade unionists and journalists. Others, such as peasants, environmental rights activists, leaders of indigenous communities, members of religious, ethnic and sexual minorities, students, teachers and intellectuals – all working for the promotion and protection of human rights – have been subjected to human rights abuses. Judges, prosecutors, members of parliament, and ombudspersons have also been targeted for upholding human rights.

Greater risks are faced by defenders whose work challenges social structures, economic interests, traditional practices and interpretations of religious precepts that may have been used over long periods of time to condone and justify violation of the human rights. Women human rights defenders are targeted by various social and private actors, such as religious groups and institutions, community or tribal elders, or even members of their own family. They become particularly vulnerable to prejudice, to exclusion and to public repudiation, not only by State forces but by social actors as well when they are engaged in the defence of women's rights.
Another category of defenders that merits more attention is that of those striving for the promotion and protection of economic social and cultural rights. Flaws in the agenda for economic development, pursued by many states, are amply reflected in the growing poverty and social exclusion of large sectors of the population in many parts of the world. These have resulted in serious violations of economic, social and cultural rights. Those affected find that in the current environment of globalization their own governments are either unable or unwilling to redress the difficulties they confront. Exploitation of labour and depletion of the environment are some of the serious forms of violations resulting from the current economic arrangements in some countries.

There are several examples when coercive power of the State has been used against human rights defenders, at times at the instigation or pressure of powerful economic interests. Leaders of indigenous and other minority communities, leaders of movements of the poor, environmental, land rights and anti-globalisation activists, trade union leaders and defenders of the rights of displaced persons, migrants and refugees are increasingly being targeted. Peaceful public action or protest against the denial of economic, social and cultural rights in several countries of Asia, for instance, have resulted in state action in violation of civil and political rights, such as freedom of association, expression and assembly, physical security and liberty. Such actions of states have caused increased public resentment against authorities. In addition, they have diminished the space for dialogue on reconciling economic policies with people's right to a safe environment, to control over their own resources, and to labour practices free of exploitation. In many parts of the world such trends have created human rights crises that find little international attention, and have seldom aroused any international concern.

It is true that violations of the rights of human rights defenders have occurred in all countries, including emerging democracies and countries with long-established democratic institutions, practices and traditions. However, conditions hampering the work or security of human rights defenders are more prevalent in States where the political and institutional arrangements are weak or are explicitly undemocratic. Human rights defenders all over the world are greatly concerned about certain trends that create the conditions for more serious and sustained violations of human rights. An appreciable weakening of the rule of law has been observed in different countries where insufficient, not genuinely representative democracies prevail with little or no space for citizen participation, and without accountability or transparency. Institutions for policing and prosecution suffer from inefficiency and corruption, and the independence of the judiciaries is severely strained. Internal monitoring systems are either non-existent or have failed to enforce compliance with human rights norms in practices or policies adopted by state institutions. Political conditions and poor practices of governance adopted by a State primarily determine the degree of risk and insecurity that defenders confront in that country.

National laws in many countries do not provide a suitable legal framework for the full realisation and enjoyment of human rights. Numerous laws exist which are incompatible with international standards and have become tools for giving legitimacy to State actions that violate human rights. Despite constitutional guarantees, rights have become subject to restrictions prescribed by law. It is these restrictions and the use of powers granted under such laws that have been widely used to curb and limit the activities of human rights defenders. National security laws have been reinvigorated or imposed in the severest forms, sometimes following a declaration of martial law or a state of emergency. In many instances special laws restrict recourse to civilian courts. In some countries such laws are a permanent part of the domestic legal framework and are used to weaken the effects of any guarantees of fundamental rights.

The freedom of association is increasingly being infringed in many countries through laws and regulations that impose a wide range of restrictive conditions on the registration, management, operation and financing of non-governmental organisations. Such practices and restrictive laws have been applied to selectively deny legal status to NGOs critical of government policies and have forced defenders to continue their work without legal protection, to terminate their activities and, in some cases, even to flee their country. Restrictions imposed on freedom of assembly have been liberally applied to prohibit or disrupt peaceful human rights assemblies, frequently on the pretext of maintenance of public order, and increasingly relying on counter-terrorism legislation and mechanisms that are not compatible with the norms of human rights and the rule of law. Defenders have been prosecuted under laws that allow the executive to arbitrarily ban public gatherings generally, or at specified locations. Farmers have been prosecuted in anti-terrorist courts for protesting attempts by State security forces to evict them from land. Villagers demonstrating against mega-projects that threaten their environment and livelihood have been charged with conducting anti-State activities. Peace activists and anti-war protesters have been maligned and threatened with prosecution.

In the current global climate, armed conflict, political tensions, struggles for the right of self-determination and movements for establishing or restoring democracy, form the backdrop for the work of human rights defenders in many countries. Governments in more and more countries are seeking to impose public order by repressing popular movements and quelling the voices of protest against the violation of rights. Upholding human rights and fundamental freedoms is being portrayed in a number of countries as a threat to national and international security. Against this stark reality, human rights defenders are finding themselves under siege. Peaceful pro-independence activists are being portrayed as disseminators of propaganda likely to harm the State, as a threat to national security, as attempting to overthrow the Government and as aiding and abetting terrorism. While falsely equating legitimate and peaceful advocacy of the right to self-determination with terrorism – however defined – is not a new phenomenon, it is certainly assuming a greater resonance now, and human rights defenders working for the realization of peoples' peaceful quests for self-determination are experiencing some of their darkest hours.

There is no denying that the menace of terrorism poses a serious threat to peace and security. Acts of terrorism have frequently targeted human rights defenders advocating the promotion and protection of human rights. Those striving for the rights of minorities or women, advancing the cause of religious tolerance and accommodation of ethnic or racial diversity, or resisting trends of ultra-nationalism have been some of the first victims of forms of extremism that have become the major cause of terrorism. It is, nevertheless, also true that human rights defenders are in the front line to combat these trends in order to preserve the norms of peace and democracy, as conditions that are fundamental for the promotion, protection and enjoyment of human rights. Their struggle against terrorism precedes the events of 11 September 2001, in New York, and has been a visible human rights activity in parts of the world where the roots of terrorism are strongest. Yet it is these defenders who have become the leading voices in pointing out that many anti-terrorism laws, and other measures, are eroding human rights norms, and are insisting that the imperative of security will not be served by violating human rights and can best be achieved within compliance of these standards. When societies fail to challenge the misconceived idea of a trade-off between security and human rights most often they get neither, and minorities and other vulnerable groups pay the price. Such notions have resulted in an assault on rule of law and human rights and are likely to become more and more entrenched if the current trends are not halted.

Human rights defenders have detected a direct connection between the severity of human rights violations and the expanding role of the military in some countries of the region. This has allowed the military sector to gain influence and encroach upon political spaces, especially when the military is in control of governance. It has also had its effects on the capacity of civil societies to develop. Serious forms of abuse have been detected during military operations carried out in response to security concerns or government campaigns against crime. Particular areas are designated as zones of military operation, barring any independent monitoring or observation of state action. Special powers conferred on the military have often dispensed with fair judicial procedures or any civilian control over their operations. It is now well documented that, with the exception of the police, military and State intelligence agencies by far outnumber others as perpetrators of abuse against human rights defenders. In view of the adverse effects of militarism on human rights activity and the high level of immunity that the military enjoys this trend is seen as a serious threat to the promotion of and protection of human rights in several countries.

Under these conditions human rights standards suffer derogation because of the imposition of a completely separate system of checks and balances and of justice. Accountability and transparency is seriously impaired. Freedom of movement and assembly, and access to information is particularly affected in such situations. Such an environment further contributes to impunity for human rights violations. Evidence of rape, torture, deaths in custody, extra-judicial executions and disappearances is well documented. Most of these violations result directly from the operations and intelligence and surveillance activities carried out by the military, and some because of the criminal activity of individual soldiers.

Even when civilian authority has been established or re-established, military presence still dominates the structures of authority and democratic culture becomes difficult to promote. It has been noted that in some countries national human rights institutions have not been given powers to investigate allegations of excesses committed by members of armed forces. There are also reports of armed forces systematically failing to comply with court orders concerning arbitrary actions that violate human rights. The military's continued lack of accountability is being questioned and there is a greater demand for transparency and public scrutiny of allegations of abuse by the military. This will become possible only if the measures and mechanisms allow comprehensive monitoring of actions and operations of military and security forces in order to prevent human rights violations.

As the Special Representative of the United Nations Secretary General on the Situation of Human Rights Defenders, an analysis of information I received from conflict and post conflict countries, highlighted the important role that human rights defenders play in restoring or maintaining peace and security. These countries and regions include the Democratic Republic of the Congo, the Sudan, the Middle East, including the Occupied Palestinian Territories, and Haiti – four situations that have been on the agenda of the Security Council in the past few years. In situations of crises, defenders can monitor an overall situation, rapidly investigate allegations of possible violations and report their conclusions, providing a measure of accountability. They also provide the international community with some independent verification of what is actually happening within an emergency situation, informing the process of taking decisions on possible actions. Because human rights defenders advocate for a peaceful solution to political, ethnic and social tensions that have the potential to break out into armed conflict, their reports and activities serve as a functional early warning system. In fact, an increase in attacks against human rights defenders in a country can in itself become an early warning for the international community. In post conflict situations defenders have played a critical role in sustaining peace and strengthening the prospects for promotion and protection of human rights in post-conflict societies.

The analysis has also highlighted the urgent need to find effective means for the protection of human rights defenders. In conflict situations human rights defenders become particularly vulnerable and are disproportionately affected. In the aftermath of widespread human rights violations that often accompany armed conflict and other civil strife, human rights defenders act on behalf of victims demanding justice for past abuses. As a result, human rights defenders are targeted by groups who, because of their involvement in past violations, are opposed to demands for accountability. Strengthening and protecting human rights defenders is therefore an important contribution to transitional justice efforts, and thereby to sustainable peace and security.

Independence, credibility and transparency are cornerstones of the efforts to promote and protect human rights. Repressive action by the State against human rights activity affects the transparency and openness with which human rights defenders can work. Such circumstances increase the risks for defenders and can undermine the credibility of their work. On their part human rights defenders must also be fully conscious that transparency, objectivity, non-partisanship and accuracy in the communication of information are essential elements of all activities in which they engage. It is only through these qualities that defenders can maintain respect for their work and withstand any attempts to discredit them, or undermine their public image.

As a response to the deteriorating situation of human rights defenders, the United Nations adopted the Declaration[1] on human rights defenders in 1998. On the one hand this was recognition of the dangers that human rights defenders confront and, on the other, a step taken by the international community to create norms for the protection of human rights activity. The Declaration has given the civil society a "role and responsibility in safeguarding democracy, promoting human rights and fundamental freedoms and contributing to the promotion and advancement of democratic societies, institutions and processes". Human rights defenders can only fulfil this responsibility effectively if they have a secure and enabling environment in which to function. Any commitment to the defence of human rights must, therefore, be tested on the basis of the degree of security that human rights defenders have in carrying out their work in all parts of the world.

The Declaration makes it the primary responsibility of the State not only to guarantee the safety of human rights defenders, but also to ensure that conditions exist in which they can carry out their activities. States must, therefore, take all possible measures to create an environment conducive to the defence of human rights. Public support for the activities of human

---

[1] The Declaration on the Rights and Responsibility of Individuals, Groups and Organs of Society to Promote and Protect Universally Recognized Human Rights and Fundamental Freedoms, adopted by the UN General Assembly on 9 December 1998, UN Doc. A/RES/53/114.

rights defenders is in itself an important means of protection for them. This support can be generated and enhanced by increasing public awareness and understanding of their work. The media can play an important role in mobilizing public opinion in support of human rights defenders and in providing information on the Declaration.

The United Nations also needs to ensure full implementation of the Declaration by a more active protection of defenders. In the preamble to the Declaration, the General Assembly recognized the relationship between international peace and security and the enjoyment of human rights. By exercising their right to promote and to strive for the protection and realization of human rights, defenders play an important role in the promotion of peace and security. When defenders are silenced and prevented from undertaking their activities, the goals of protecting peace, security and human rights are seriously undermined. In spite of their essential role, the protection of human rights defenders and their work is still not adequately emphasized within the United Nations system. The UN Security Council resolutions on some of the situations that it has dealt with mention the protection of humanitarian workers, but no resolution of the Security Council talks about the protection of human rights defenders. I believe this is an omission that must be corrected by the Security Council in its future decisions.

Civil Society initiatives for support of human rights defenders are already having a visible impact. Creation of coalitions, national and regional networks for communication of information, monitoring groups and support groups is a development that is extremely reassuring. These networks are in themselves mechanisms for the protection of human rights defenders. Taking practical steps to protect persecuted defenders should be an important part of the responsibilities of coalitions. Urgent action networks are already functioning at the national, region and international levels and should be utilized more widely as a mechanism for the protection of human rights defenders. Regional initiatives to create monitoring groups and evacuation teams to respond immediately in situations where human rights defenders are in grave and imminent danger can strengthen the element of protection.

Special attention must be paid to the safety of human rights defenders from marginalized segments of society, as they are more vulnerable to risk. Better access must be provided to those working in remote areas for gathering and disseminating information. Human rights defenders in exile are especially vulnerable and should be supported by the human rights community at the regional level, so that they are able to continue their work from outside.

International human rights law gives recognition to and establishes the principles and standards for the protection, promotion and realization of human rights and fundamental freedoms. Inherent in this protection is the guarantee that activities for the promotion and protection of these rights can be conducted without fear and hindrance. While proclaiming the Universal Declaration of Human Rights (UDHR), the UN General Assembly bound every individual and every organ of the society to strive for the promotion of respect for these rights and freedoms[2]. This is the beginning of the evolution of the right to defend human rights. Human rights defenders are central to the realization of this right. It is only through consolidated and well-coordinated efforts of governments, NGOs and the international communities that we can ensure that these defenders can carry out their activities with safety and facility.

---

[2] See the last paragraph of the Preamble to the Universal Declaration of Human Rights.

6th Annual Theo van Boven Lecture

Maastricht University

25 November 2015

Introduction

In 2015 the theme of the annual Theo van Boven lecture was Contemporary Forms of Slavery. This is a current problem today, not only in developing countries, but also in developed countries all over the world. One may think of children in African countries who work on cocoa bean plantations, but also involuntary employed domestic workers in the Gulf region and forced prostitution in European countries. The lecture was delivered by Prof. Jean Allain, a renowned international expert on the legal aspects of slavery. In his lecture Prof. Allain focused on the role and responsibility of human rights scholars to address contemporary forms of slavery by studying the legal history of the concept of slavery. The presentation by Prof. Allain was followed by a response from Dr. Aidan McQuade, Director of Anti-Slavery International, a leading human rights NGO. In his reaction Mr. McQuade, from a more practical perspective, dealt with the relationship between contemporary forms of slavery, political power positions, political will and the 2015 UN Sustainable Development Goals.

Prof. Jean Allain holds the Chair in Public International Law at Queen's University, Belfast. He is a generalist in public international law with a specialisation in human rights and is the leading legal expert on issues of slavery and trafficking. He is also the Director of the Human Rights Centre of Queen's University. In 2015, Prof. Allain was appointed Special Adviser to Anti-Slavery International. Prof. Allain's recent publications include: Jean Allain, *The Law and Slavery: Prohibiting Human Exploitation*, Martinus Nijhoff, 2015, 640 pp.

Dr. Aidan McQuade is Director of Anti-Slavery International, the oldest international human rights organisation in the world, founded in London in 1839, which works to eliminate all forms of slavery around the world. He graduated from Queen's University Belfast with a civil engineering degree and then worked in Ethiopia for Concern and Caritas Switzerland, Médecins Sans Frontières Holland in Afghanistan and Oxfam in Angola before taking up the post at Anti-Slavery International in 2006.

Slavery and the Human Rights Scholars

Jean Allain

It is too often repeated that "it is an honour" when invited to give a talk; and yet for me the invitation to give the Theo van Boven Lecture this evening touches me deeply, as for me it is both a vindication of my work carried out in splendid isolation, with very little contact with the invisible college of international lawyers; and a recognition of which I am the proudest: recognition based on the merits of its scholarly value.

I welcome the opportunity of this Lecture to present to a number of individuals that I rate very highly in regard to their work around issues of international human rights law including, foremost Theo van Boven, whose work as the Director of the Human Rights Division within the United Nations and later in his capacity of both Special Rapporteur on the Right to Reparation to Victims of Gross Violations of Human Rights and Special Rapporteur related to Torture came to be at the centre of what we now take for granted: an international framework of human rights norms and protection and a growing number of societies where human rights are culturally embedded.[1] So, I trust you will understand that it is deeply gratifying for me to say: it is an honour to be here this evening to present the 2015 Theo van Boven Lecture.

I wish to extend my gratitude to the Maastricht Centre for Human Rights and more specifically to its Director, Professor Fons Coomans, for inviting me this evening and for his hospitality. Prof Coomans' scholarship on issues of human rights, both in its breadth and substance, speaks to the honour I feel in having received this invitation adds that much more to the feelings I hold this evening.

The Role of Human Rights Scholars

This evening I wish to consider with you what it means to be a scholar of international human rights law – an academic writer who specialises in issues of human rights – what responsibilities that entails, and wish to sketch out for you my work on contemporary forms of slavery to demonstrate how fundamental historical and archival research is to establishing a scholarly

---

[1] Consider three books published in 2012 which consider the evolution of international human rights: A. Iriye, P. Goedde and W. Hitchcock (eds.), *The Human Rights Revolution: An International History*; Samuel Moyn, *The Last Utopia: Human Rights in History*; and Aryeh Neier, *The International Human Rights Movement: A History*.

basis upon which to advance knowledge in the area of international human rights law.

The role of the human rights scholar is, in advancing knowledge, an obligation to question not only perceived wisdoms, to take nothing for granted, but also to build a foundation of knowledge upon which to question those amongst that invisible college who would perpetuate myths, tropes, and historical amnesia. With that role, of course, comes a great responsibility, one which is at the heart of what we do: to be fundamentally honest in our development – some would say creation – of an alternative reality through the pen. That ultimately, in developing scholarship, we tell a story, a social construct, which should seek to mirror an historical reality in such a way as to both capture its essence and to speak to power and the oppressed in a manner which does justice to, first and foremost, human beings.

This, with the realisation that in considering human beings within a framework of international human rights law is to consider such persons within a Statist system – a system of laws which is developed for human beings but through the filter of the State. To best grasp this understanding is to recognise the fundamental paradox of international human rights law: that the law, created by States reflects the interest of States often at the expense of human beings. Consider the following example of that paradox, recognising that in law, language matters. Article 14(1) of the Universal Declaration of Human Rights reads: "Everyone has the right to seek and to enjoy in other countries asylum from persecution".

> Let me digress for a moment, to say that for many the Universal Declaration of Human Rights approaches being a sacred text – yet this view is ahistorical. For me, having done my homework and having read through the work of the United Nations Commission on Human Rights in the lead up to 1948 symbolises a lost opportunity, an opportunity to establish an international court of human rights, to establish an international treaty related to human rights, but that instead then mutated into but a declaration. As I will return to it, I might also mention here that the failure at the United Nations level to gain an international human rights instrument, spurred on Europeans to the Congress of Europe, which then led to the Council of Europe and shortly thereafter the European Human Rights Convention. So the inability to gain agreement at the United Nations level, lead to movement at the European level.

Returning now from my excursion: If we look at the provisions of Article 14(1), upon our first reading and understanding that the object and purpose of the Declaration is to provide rights protection to human beings, one would be forgiven for believing that the right to asylum is a right vested in the person. Yet, read those provisions once more: "everyone has a right to seek [...] asylum from persecution", and "everyone has a right to [...] enjoy [...] asylum from persecution". What is missing from this equation is that everyone has a right of asylum. In other words, human beings have the right to seek asylum and, once granted, to enjoy asylum, but they do not have a right to asylum; rather it is in the gift – a right – of the State to give asylum. Thus, if we are intellectually honest we recognise that there is no human right to asylum, rather there is a State right to asylum.

With this recognition of the Statist environment which we work in, there is a propensity for human rights lawyers to push the boundaries. Most evidently this has transpired with regard to the regime we now have within the UN human rights system: the development of general comments/recommendations for instance; the development of treaty supervisory bodies and their reporting requirements; the growth of special procedures mandates, and even the UPR: Universal Periodic Review. Likewise, the regional systems – the African, European and Inter-American – have progressively developed the law of human rights.

What I wish to argue here is not so much against pushing against boundaries, rather for the legal scholar – as opposed legal practitioner or human rights lawyer – that the pushing of boundaries must take place from a position of authority. Authority, not vested in the person – in the individual – rather authority developed through one's scholarship. This is not to speak against a Scelleian notion of *dédoublement fonctionnel* but to recognise that when we wear a second hat – as an advocate, as a commissioned writer, or as an expert working in our individual capacity – that it is by virtue of our primary role as scholar.[2] And that role is scholarship.

Where scholarship is concerned, the study of international human rights law raises fundamental constraints that are endemic of the nature of international law and its lack of a central adjudicative arm and the of lack obligatory adjudication. The result is that there is limited jurisprudence in the traditional sense, which emerges from international human rights law. Here I am thinking primarily of the United Nations system, where individual petitions are considered by quasi-judicial organs – those treaty monitoring bodies already mentioned, such as the Committee on the Rights of the Child. The result of this is that in seeking to consider international human rights law – as international human right law, rather than say its application at the domestic level – there is very little to hang one's hat on. And yet, we should recognise that sound scholarship requires the development of strong foundations in considering the law and that in the context we work in, the best peg at our disposal is to read the law in context – a context born from the evolution of those provisions in law. What I am arguing for, and the fundamental lesson that I bring with me tonight then, is that the foundations of legal analysis within international human rights law must be drawn from the historical evolution of the normative content of those provisions with which we wish to engage.

---

2   Antonio Cassese, "Remarks on Scelle's Theory of "Role Splitting" (*dédoublement fonctionnel*) in International Law", [1990] 1 *European Journal of International Law* 210.

Contemporary Forms of Slavery

So, let me turn to consider issues of contemporary forms of slavery so as to demonstrate the richness which can lie in the archives in Geneva; but also the pitfalls of being ahistorical. *This with the recognition that 10 years ago, the overall regime of contemporary forms of slavery was in complete disarray, its provision in law effectively dead-letter.*

What I propose to do this evening is to touch lightly on examples related to the slave trade, to servitude, and to forced labour to show the role of the legal scholar in international human rights, before focusing on the manner in which my work has led to a breakthrough in regard to the application of the law to instances of contemporary slavery.

The Slave Trade and the Myth of Universal Jurisdiction

One of the lingering, often repeated, myths which touches on the area I have researched was most recently expressed by now Judge James Crawford of the International Court of Justice, in his 2012 edition of *Brownlie's Principles of Public International Law*, where he notes that there was universal jurisdiction over the slave trade allowing, like piracy, the ability for any State to suppress it on the high seas.[3] This, as I have pointed in the pages of the *American Journal of International Law* in a review of Jenny Martinez's 2012 *The Slave Trade and the Origins of International Human Rights Law*, goes against a well-established historical record of failed attempts to equate the slave trade to piracy in international law and establish universal jurisdiction. This objective, set by the Government of the United Kingdom was tenaciously pursued from the era of the Concert of Europe; through the 1890 Brussels Conference (where an agreed zone in the Indian Ocean was delineated as a location where the slave trade could be suppressed); and again during both the negotiations of the 1926 Slavery Convention and the 1956 Supplementary Convention; and, in depth, as part of the move to establish the 1958 High Seas and 1982 Law of the Sea conventions.[4]

For its part, the United Nations International Law Commission considered this very issue from 1950 onwards in its considerations of the regime of the

---

3   James Crawford, *Brownlie's Principles of Public International Law*, 2012, p. 468 where he writes: "The original crime to which universal jurisdiction attached was that of piracy *ius gentium*, which was in turn followed by slavery".

4   See my chapter on the slave trade in Jean Allain, *Slavery in International Law: Of Human Exploitation and Trafficking*, 2013, pp. 57–104; and more generally, Jean Allain "Nineteenth Century Law of the Sea and the British Abolition of the Slave Trade", *British Yearbook of International Law*, Vol. 78, 2008, pp. 342–388.

high seas. The Special Rapporteur, Mr. J.P.A. François, set out the state of play of applicable law:

> If the slave trade were regarded as an act of piracy, any vessel suspected of the offence could be stopped by any warship and conducted to one of the latter's ports to be tried by the national courts. Part at least of the ground for internationalizing the crime of piracy is that the acts occur on the high seas and that in many cases there are no relations between the pirates and a given country. The slave trade, on the other hand, takes place between two given countries. Since both these countries are bound to co-operate in repressing the slave trade, internationalization – meaning that the vessel may be conducted to any port for trial by the local courts – does not appear appropriate.[5]

François then concluded:

> States were not prepared to go nearly so far in the case of the slave trade as in the case of piracy. In the one case [re: the slave trade] they had limited the right of approach to specified zones, but not in the other. [The Special Rapporteur] did not think that the two questions could be lumped together, unless the law governing the slave trade were substantially widened, in which case the Commission would no longer be codifying existing law.[6]

The Commission followed François' lead, which is now codified through separate provisions of the 1982 Law of the Sea Convention, as related to the seizing pirate ships and Article 110 touching on limited right to board ships suspected of involvement in the slave trade. This latter provision reinforces the national jurisdiction of flag States, as visits are only allowed to ascertain the fraudulent use of such flags, not to suppress the slave trade, this falling exclusively within the jurisdiction of the flag State, rather than the myth of universal jurisdiction.[7]

The Trope of Forced Labour as a Jus Cogens Norm

In 2014, my work flirted once more with *jus cogens*, as the Legal Adviser of the International Labour Organisation, at the Conference negotiating a Protocol to the Forced Labour Convention, sought to argue that the prohibition of

---

5   United Nations, General Assembly, International Law Commission, Second Report of the High Seas by J.P.A. François, Rapporteur, UN Doc A/CN.4/42, 10 April 1951, p. 26.
6   International Law Commission, Yearbook of the International Law Commission, 21 October 1957, UN Doc. A/CN.4/SER.A/1951, 350.
7   See Articles 105 and 110, United Nations Law of the Sea Convention, 1982.

forced labour was of *jus cogens* norm.[8] This myth, first perpetuated in the 1998 Report of the ILO Commission of Inquiry into issues of forced labour in Myanmar gained currency both within the Organisation and beyond, was laid to rest in Geneva in 2014.[9] This myth was created by less than a "mastery of the principles of international law", as it sought to ride the coattails of a reading of *slavery as a concept* which included not only slavery, but also servitude, and more importantly for our purposes: forced labour.[10] While I will consider the evolution of the move towards slavery, servitude and forced labour as legally defined rather than as a concept later, for now, it should be recognised that forced labour cannot meet the threshold of a *jus cogens* norm, as it is not peremptory: as built into its very definition are exceptions (re: permissible derogations) related to penal labour, military service, emergency assistance, "civic obligations" and the archaic, colonial, "communal services". It should be emphasised that it is these exceptions – recognised by the ILO Expert Committee as forms of forced labour – that were the stumbling block which prevented forced labour from being included in the pithy provisions of the 1948 Universal Declaration of Human Rights.[11]

At the negotiations of the 2014 Protocol to the 1930 Forced Labour Convention, the draft included a preambular provision which read: "that the prohibition of forced or compulsory labour should be considered a peremptory norm of international law". Taking up my analysis developed previously, the member of the Canadian delegation was unwilling to support that amendment as "she had been advised that this could only apply to provisions or rights that had no

---

[8] See Jean Allain, "The *Jus cogens* Nature of *Non-Refoulement*", International Journal of Refugee Law, Vol. 13, 2001, pp. 533–558; which led to the following, first published independently 2001, then after as: Sir Elihu Lauterpacht and Daniel Bethlehem "*The Scope and Content of the Principle of Non-Refoulement: Opinion*", Erika Feller et al., eds., Refugee Protection in International Law: UNHCR's Global Consultations on International Protection, 2003; and the Council of the International Institute of Humanitarian Law, Sanremo Declaration on the Principle of Non-Refoulement, September 2001.

[9] See International Labour Organisation, Governing Body, Forced Labour in Myanmar (Burma), Report of the Commission of Inquiry appointed under article 26 of the Constitution of the International Labour Organization to examine the observance by Myanmar of the Forced Labour Convention, 1930 (No. 29), 2 July 1998, para. 203; repeated in International Labour Organisation, Report for Discussion at the Tripartite Meeting of Experts Concerning The Possible Adoption of an ILO Instrument to Supplement the Forced Labour Convention, 1930 (No.29), TMELE/2013, 2013, p. 3; and noted in *John Doe 1 v. Unocal Corporation*, United States Court of Appeals, Ninth Circuit 395 F.3d 932 (2002).

[10] See Jean Allain, *The Law and Slavery: Prohibiting Human Exploitation*, 2015, pp. 234–238.

[11] See International Labour Conference, 65th Session, Item III, Report of the Committee of Experts on the Application of Conventions and Recommendations, General Survey on the Reports Relating to Forced Labour Convention, 1930 (NO. 29), and the Abolition of Forced Labour Convention, 1957 (No. 105), Report III (Part 4B), 1979, pp. 9–10.

lawful derogations, which was not the case for forced labour". Despite the Legal Adviser of the ILO stating that "prohibition of forced labour could be considered a peremptory norm of international law – indeed this had been the position taken by ILO supervisory bodies"; the proposal was withdrawn as a result of hesitation by European Union States.[12]

Servitude and Historical Amnesia

It should be recognised that "servitude" as a legal concept has had little impact on international human rights law, brought on by a lack of engagement and an inability of courts to provide guidance so as to develop a normative space between slavery or forced labour. In 2005, the European Court of Human Rights provided what remains the fullest consideration of the parameters of servitude: "servitude means an obligation to provide one's services that is imposed by the use of coercion, and is to be linked with the concept of slavery".[13] This hardly moves the agenda forward. And yet, the agenda of understanding the legal parameters of servitude has languished – suffering an historical amnesia, as academics have failed to engage with the term.[14]

However, for those who would bother looking, the historical record provides both an understanding of the term and a means of engaging with it in such a manner as to bring that concept to life. Simply put, servitude are those "institutions and practices similar to slavery" as set out in the 1956 Supplementary Convention on the Abolition of Slavery, the Slave Trade, and Institutions and Practices Similar to Slavery, which until its penultimate draft in 1956 was entitled the "A Supplementary Convention on Slavery and Other Forms of Servitude".[15] The felt-need to replace the term servitude with that of, what is often referred to as, "practices similar to slavery", was an unwillingness on the part of the Soviet Union to follow the lead of the 1948 Universal Declaration of Human Rights which called for the abolition of

---

12 International Labour Conference, 103th Session, Provisional Record, Report of the Committee on Forced Labour, Fourth Item on the Agenda: Supplementing The Force Labour Convention 1930(No. 29), To Address Implementation Gaps to Advance Prevention, Protection and Compensation Measures, To Effectively Achieve the Elimination of Forced Labour, Number 9, 8 June 2014, pp. 9–15, paras. 66, 68, 75, 76, and 79; see also: Jean Allain, "The Implications of the Preparatory Works for Debates on Slavery, Servitude and Forced Labour", Adelle Blackett and Anne Trebilcock (eds.), *Research Handbook on Transnational Labour Law*, 2015, pp 532–535.

13 *Siliadin v. France*, ECHR, 26 July 2005,para 124.

14 See, for instance, Cherif Bassiouni and Ved Nanda, "The Crime of Slavery and Slave Trade", Cherif Bassiouni, *Crimes against Humanity in International Criminal Law*, 1999.

15 United Nations, Economic and Social Council, Report of the Ad Hoc Committee on Slavery (Second Session), UN Doc E/1998, E/AC.33/13, 4 May 1951, p. 31.

servitude. Instead, the Soviet Representative on the Committee drafting the Supplementary Convention managed to expunge the very term "servitude" from the substance of the proposed instrument meant to deal precisely with that issue and which had been considered since 1922 under the rubrics of "servitude". Instead of heeding the clarion call of the Universal Declaration and abolishing servitude, the drafters of the 1956 Convention developed a new term so as to provide them with the diplomatic cover when agreeing not to abolish servitude but to end it "progressively and as soon as possible".[16]

As a result, it should be recognised that the institutions and practices set out in Article 1 of the 1956 Supplementary Convention are, in fact, conventional servitudes. The 1956 Convention lists these as debt bondage, serfdom, and in my language: servile marriage (i.e.: bridal sale, wife transfer, and widow inheritance), and child exploitation. As a result of this reading, the normative space which captures servitude is, in law, quite narrow, as both serfdom and servile marriage, as defined, meet – as the UN Secretary-General alluded to in 1953 – the definition of slavery. As for child exploitation, the original negotiation process effectively rendered that provision inoperative; however, it was given a new life by its development in the 2000 Optional Protocol to the Convention on the Rights of the Child so as to now deal with the "sale of children", and thus also meet the threshold of slavery.[17] This leaves us with debt bondage as servitude:

> the status or condition arising from a pledge by a debtor of his personal services or of those of a person under his control as security for a debt, if the value of those services as reasonably assessed is not applied towards

---

16 See Jean Allain, "On the Curious Disappearance of Human Servitude from General International Law", 11 *Journal of the History Of International Law* 303 (2009); and Jean Allain, "The International Legal Regime of Slavery and Human Exploitation and its Obfuscation by the Term of Art: "Slavery-Like Practice"", *Cahiers de la recherche en droits fondamentaux*, Vol. 10, 2012, pp. 27–42, both reproduced in Jean Allain, *The Law and Slavery: Prohibiting Human Exploitation*, 2015, pp. 297–396 and 159–193. More general see my chapter on "Servitude or Practices Similar to Slavery" in Jean Allain, *Slavery in International Law: Of Human Exploitation and Trafficking*, 2013, pp. 143–202.

17 Article 1 of the 1956 Supplementary Convention on the Abolition of Slavery, the Slave Trade, and Institutions and Practices Similar to Slavery reads:
Each of the States Parties to this Convention shall take all practicable and necessary legislative and other measures to bring about progressively and as soon as possible the complete abolition or abandonment of the following institutions and practices, where they still exist and whether or not they are covered by the definition of slavery contained in article 1 of the Slavery Convention signed at Geneva on 25 September 1926:
(a) Debt bondage, that is to say, the status or condition arising from a pledge by a debtor of his personal services or of those of a person under his control as security for a debt, if the value of those services as reasonably assessed is not applied towards the

the liquidation of the debt or the length and nature of those services are not respectively limited and defined.

While this reading leaves limited normative space for servitude, it moves beyond the academic ignorance which had existed previously and provides the legal certainty to allow courts to go beyond their struggle to give content to the established international human right not to be held in servitude by recognising that it is, in law, debt bondage.

The Legal Substance of Slavery

In my most recent book, the 2015 *The Law of Slavery* – which gathers together my disparate articles, book review, case briefs and public lectures into one volume so as to provide an all-encompassing collection of works that were the basis of 2013 *Slavery in International Law* – I devote one of four sections

---

liquidation of the debt or the length and nature of those services are not respectively limited and defined;

(b) Serfdom, that is to say, the condition or status of a tenant who is by law, custom or agreement bound to live and labour on land belonging to another person and to render some determinate service to such other person, whether for reward or not, and is not free to change his status;

(c) Any institution or practice whereby:
  (i) A woman, without the right to refuse, is promised or given in marriage on payment of a consideration in money or in kind to her parents, guardian, family or any other person or group; or
  (ii) The husband of a woman, his family, or his clan, has the right to transfer her to another person for value received or otherwise; or
  (iii) A woman on the death of her husband is liable to be inherited by another person;

(d) Any institution or practice whereby a child or young person under the age of 18 years is delivered by either or both of his natural parents or by his guardian to another person, whether for reward or not, with a view to the exploitation of the child or young person or of his labour.

With regard to the United Nations Secretary-General, he echoed the findings of the *Ad Hoc Committee on Slavery* in his 1953 Report noting, that where debt bondage, forced marriage and child trafficking were concerned, "in the main these institutions or practices are covered" by the definition of slavery found in the 1926 Slavery Convention". United Nations Economic and Social Council, Slavery, the Slave Trade, and other forms of Servitude (Report of the Secretary-General), UN Doc. E/2357, 27 January 1953, p. 27.

For the provision related to sale of children, see Article 2 (a), Optional Protocol to the Convention on the Rights of the Child on the Sale of Children, Child Prostitution and Child Pornography, 2000.

to "Challenging the Status Quo". Through this specific collection of works, I sought to deconstruct the contemporary thinking which prevailed on issues of forced labour, servitude, slavery, the slave trade, and trafficking – while simultaneously building up a foundation of knowledge which has allowed for the construction not only a new, but maybe more importantly, a *coherent*, narrative around issues of contemporary slavery.[18]

In the year 2002 I had completed drafting a study entitled *International Law in the Middle East*, and sought to consider a new area of the law to investigate. I do recall that the choice had been between slavery and enclaves in international law. The ultimate choice, in many ways, however, was pre-ordained by a trip to Ghana in 2000 and a visit to the so-called "slave castles" at Elmina and Cape Coast. This visit piqued an interest in the slave trade that in turn had me read about its history. What I very quickly came to realise, was that the issue of the slave trade and more generally slavery had, over the last 40 years, moved from the peripheries of historical study which had allowed W.E.H. Lecky to paint British abolition as "among the three or four perfectly virtuous pages comprised in this history of nations"; to the centre, and made up one of the most vibrant and engaged areas for History departments the world over.[19] It was a time in which this generation of the scholars, people such as Brion Davies, Drescher, Engerman, Patterson and Miers, were moving to produce synthesis works by developing their accumulative knowledge into monograph form.[20]

---

18 The pieces in the section on "Challenging the Status Quo" found in *The Law and Slavery: Prohibiting Human Exploitation*, 2015, first appears as: a review of "Kevin Bales, *Understanding Global Slavery: A Reader*, 2005" (2008) 20 *International Journal of Refugee Law* 228, "Silvia Scarpa, *Trafficking in Human Beings: Modern Slavery*, 2008" (2009) 20 *European Journal of International Law* 453, "Brennan Fernne and John Packer (eds.), "Colonialism, Slavery, Reparations and Trade: Remedying the Past?, 2012", (2012) 7 *Irish Yearbook of International Law* 305, and "Jenny Martinez, *The Slave Trade and the Origins of International Human Rights Law*" (2012) 107 *American Journal of International Law* 109; the cases notes: "*Hadijatou Mani Koraou v. Republic of Niger*" (2009) 103 *American Journal of International Law* 311, and "*Rantsev v. Cyprus and Russia*: The European Court of Human Rights and Trafficking as Slavery", (2010) 10 *Human Rights Law Review* 546; as well as "Immanent Critique: International Law and the Dubious Case-Law on Slavery" a paper presented at The Wilberforce Institute for the Study of Slavery and Emancipation (WISE), May 2009; and the journal article: "No Effective Trafficking Definition Exists: Domestic Implementation of the Palermo Protocol", (2014) 7 *Albany Government Law Review* 111.
19 See Roger Anstey, *The Atlantic Slave Trade and British Abolition 1760–1810*, 1975, p. xx; where he quotes W.E.H. Lecky, *A History of European Morals*, 1884.
20 David Brion Davis, *Inhuman Bondage: The Rise and Fall of Slavery in the New World*, 2006; Seymour Drescher, *Abolition: A History of Slavery and Antislavery*, 2009; Stanley Engerman, *Slavery, Emancipation, and Freedom: Comparative Perspectives*, 2007; Orlando Patterson, *Slavery and Social Death*, and Suzanne Miers, *Slavery in the Twentieth Century*, 2003.

In 2004, my research started in earnest, as I spent time in the Archives of the League of Nations and the United Nations Library in Geneva, a place familiar to me as a result of my doctoral studies at the Graduate Institute of International Studies (HEI), University of Geneva. I spent a relatively short period this first visit, as I busied myself photographic material fundamental to undertaking my study of the international move to abolish what I term *human exploitation*: forced labour, servitude, the slave trade, slavery, and trafficking. Over the following two years I worked through that material, and quickly came to realise that I had been systematically drafting the legislative history of provisions related to slavery and the slave trade found in the 1926 Slavery Convention and 1956 Supplementary Convention – The Supplementary Convention on the Abolition of Slavery, the Slave Trade, and Institutions and Practices Similar to Slavery. With this in hand, I approached Martinus Nijhoff – the venerable Dutch publishing house of international law texts – and we agreed that I would produce, as I in fact did in 2008, the *travaux préparatoires* of these instruments.[21]

While that book was in its page-proof stage in early 2008, and on the basis of a presentation I had made of my research at the International Criminal Court, as part of Office of the Prosecutor's Guest Lecture Series, the Australian Human Rights and Equal Opportunity Commission contacted me and asked whether my research had progress beyond my 2007 Lecture. On the basis of having considered the proofs I supplied them, they wrote back to say they would be intervening in what would become the *Tang* case, which took my research and started the momentum towards establishing the definition of slavery, that was introduced in the 1926 Slavery Conventions, as being applicable to cases of contemporary slavery.

The *Tang* case provided for a paradigm shift as it was the culmination of a process, which transpired through the Australian court system, of debunking the status quo myth that slavery was a concept rather than defined in law. The culmination of this myth, first propagated by the 1930 International Commission of Inquiry into the Existence of Slavery and Forced Labour in the Republic of Liberia, was last disseminated within the United Nations through a 2000 Working Paper of the then Sub-Commission on the Promotion and Protection of Human Right prepared by David Weissbrodt – and it should be said – Anti-Slavery International. It was Weissbrodt's opinion that "In order for the United Nations or any other international body to carry out a mandate concerned with slavery effectively, it is necessary to develop an international consensus on what practices are included within the *concept* of slavery."[22] For Weissbrodt, these practices included serfdom, forced labour, debt bondage,

---

21 See Jean Allain, *The Slavery Conventions: The Travaux Préparatoires of the 1926 League of Nations Convention and the 1956 United Nations Convention*, Martinus Nijhoff, 2008.

22 United Nations, Sub-Commission on the Promotion and Protection of Human Right, *Contemporary Forms of Slavery: Updated review of the implementation of and follow-up to*

migrant workers, trafficking, prostitution, forced marriage and sale of wives, and child labour and child servitude.

As I will explain, my work in developing an understanding of the law specifically around slavery has been to move away from slavery as a concept, or manifest in various forms and rather to consider the substance of the relationship at hand. That approach was effectively endorsed first by the Court of Appeal of the Supreme Court of Victoria, in Australia, which noted that:

> The understanding of the scope of the definition of slavery stated by Jean Allain is at odds with that of David Weissbrodt in his paper commissioned by the Office of the United Nations High Commissioner for Human Rights. Weissbrodt concluded that the definition was intended to include the broader range of practices that had been addressed by the Temporary Slavery Commission of 1924, including debt bondage, serfdom, practices involving restrictions of liberty and personal control analogous to slavery, practices such as acquisition of women and girls in the guise of payment of dowry, and so forth. It was not limited to chattel slavery, but required examination of the degree of restriction and control exercised over the person, rather than concentration on the criterion of ownership.[23]

The Supreme Court concluded that "in final analysis, it is unnecessary to resolve the dispute between Allain and Weissbrodt"; however, the equivalent of the Australian Supreme Court – the High Court of Australia – did just that, in its 2008 *Tang* case. This was made most evident in oral proceedings when it was noted before the High Court that there "is perhaps an element of advocacy in Mr Weissbrodt's article about the need to expand the definition of "slavery", or as Mr Allain was undertaking, a more academic task of investigating the actual *travaux préparatoires* of the 1926 Convention and the 1956 Convention as well".[24]

While a large number of States have included the prohibition against slavery within their constitutions or within legislation related to criminal or human rights law, Australia is one of a dozen States to have incorporated the 1926 definition of slavery into its domestic legal order. That definition reads:

> Slavery is the status or condition over whom any or all of the powers attaching to the right of ownership are exercised.

---

the conventions on slavery, Working Paper prepared by David Weissbrodt and Anti-Slavery International, UN Doc. E/CN.4/Sub.2/2000/3, 26 May 2000, p. 5. Emphasis added.

23   Supreme Court of Victoria (Court of Appeal), *Queen v Wei Tang*, [2007] VSCA 134, 2 July 2007, para 36.

24   High Court of Australia, *The Queen v Wei Tang*, [2008] HCA Trans 180, 14 May 2008, para 5595, p. 124.

That decision engaged both the normative content of slavery – speaking of the "antithesis of slavery is freedom" – and a juridical evolution and evaluation of the law around the definition of slavery.[25] However, beyond this; the judgment gave the imprimatur of authority to my archival research and legal analysis which demonstrated that this definition was applicable to both *de jure* slavery and *de facto* slavery; in other words to both historical and contemporary slavery.

> For those of you who have seen the Oscar-winner film *12 Years a Slave*, this distinction will be obvious, as the protagonist, Solomon Northup, was not legally enslaved – but he was indeed kept in a condition of *de facto* slavery.
>
> A further way of conceptualising this distinction is to think of torture, which having been abolished from the 18th century onwards is now prohibited in law. That said, few would argue that torture does not exist today.

What the slavery definition lacks in eloquence, it makes up for in capturing the lived experience of those enslaved, both historically and contemporaneously.

In saying this, I am not equating the historical Transatlantic Slave Trade to modern-day slavery as, in the words of Robin Blackburn in his monumental trilogy, that Trade was a different "species of slavery".[26] Rather, what I am saying is that, for the person enslaved at any time in history, the 1926 definition captures that lived experience; however, as many of you will realise, what distinguishes the present from the enslavement of the Transatlantic Slave Trade is both its industrial scale – 12.5 million people stolen from Africa – and the superstructure of racism which emerged to justify that Trade, the effects of which continues to be felt deeply amongst the African Diaspora. Beyond this, what is often forgotten is the fundamental role which the law and the legal infrastructure played in providing the space and the justification to unleash unspeakable violence towards African children, men, and women. In reclaiming that last voice, let me provide you with two simple, four-letter words which carry 500 years of brutish and uncivilised behaviour by Europeans: the whip and rape.[27]

As for the lingering effect of the *Maangamizi* – this African Holocaust –, it is most evident in the recognition in both the 2009 Durban Declaration and in the 2014 United Nations General Assembly Resolution declaring 2015 as the

---

25 *The Queen v Tang* [2008] HCA 39, 28 August 2008, para. 25.
26 Robin Blackburn, *The Overthrow of Colonial Slavery 1776–1848*, 1988, p. 7. The trilogy also includes The *Making of New World Slavery: From the Baroque to the Modern*, 1492–1800, 2010 and The *American Crucible: Slavery, Emancipation and Human Rights*, 2013.
27 Giving voice to the voiceless is the fiction of Marlon James, *The Book of Night Women*, 2009.

start of the International Decade for People of African Descent, that "people of African descent were victims of slavery, the slave trade and colonialism, and continue to be victims of their consequences".[28]

While debunking the *status quo* myth that slavery was a concept rather than defined in law, the *Tang* case also created momentum by addressing two fundamental elements, the first already noted, was with regard to the application of the 1926 definition of slavery to both situations of *de jure* and *de facto* slavery. Citing my work, the High Court noted that "[s]tatus is a legal concept" and that "the evident purpose of the reference to "condition" was to cover slavery *de facto* as well as *de jure*".[29] Behind this rather mundane determination was the genealogy which starts with the politically motivated misreading by the 1930 International Commission dealing with Liberia, of the Report related to the drafting of the 1926 Convention to the Assembly of the League of Nations.[30]
The second fundamental element which the High Court of Australia achieved in building momentum towards providing a normative basis to slavery, was to cite a passage by the United Nations Secretary-General of what constituted those "powers attaching to the right of ownership" noted in the definition. Here then is a prime example of scholarship in action. I can be bold enough to say that my archival work rescued this document from oblivion – and that it was a bit of a Eureka moment – as, working systematically, on a chronological basis, through first the archives of the League of Nations, then through the document of the Library of the United Nations in Geneva, that I had read, synthesised, and analysed, more than forty years of these Organisations"

---

28 United Nations, General Assembly, Resolution 69/16, 1 December 2014; Annex: Programme of activities for the implementation of the International Decade for People of African Descent, Paragraph 3, p. 3.
Note also the Declaration of the World Conference against Racism, Racial Discrimination, Xenophobia and Related Intolerance which reads at Paragraph 13:
We acknowledge that slavery and the slave trade, including the transatlantic slave trade, were appalling tragedies in the history of humanity not only because of their abhorrent barbarism but also in terms of their magnitude, organized nature and especially their negation of the essence of the victims, and further acknowledge that slavery and the slave trade are a crime against humanity and should always have been so, especially the transatlantic slave trade and are among the major sources and manifestations of racism, racial discrimination, xenophobia and related intolerance, and that Africans and people of African descent, Asians and people of Asian descent and indigenous peoples were victims of these acts and continue to be victims of their consequences.

29 *The Queen v Tang* [2008] HCA 39, 28 August 2008, para. 25.

30 See Jean Allain, "A Legal Consideration of "Slavery" in Light of the *Travaux Préparatoires* of the 1926 Convention", as reproduced in Jean Allain, *The Law and Slavery: Prohibiting Human Exploitation*, 2015, pp. 412–415.

consideration before that moment arrived. As I was reading through a 1953 Report of the Secretary-General to the Economic and Social Council, what I discovered in an extended footnote was what remains the only authoritative pronouncement within the United Nations system of the characteristics of various "powers attaching the right of ownership".[31]

In that footnote, the UN Secretary-General stated that the *Travaux Préparatoires* of the 1926 Convention did not provide "any precise indication of the meaning of the "power attaching to the right of ownership""; instead, Secretary-General U Thant pointed "to authority of the master over the slave in Roman law", going on to say that this "authority was of an absolute nature, comparable to the rights of ownership, which included the right to acquire, to use, or to dispose".[32] While the High Court of Australia engaged with the UN Secretary-General's consideration of powers attaching the right of ownership, it did so only to the extent required by the facts of that case.

With these elements in my pocket, I took it upon myself to build what came to be called the Research Network on the Legal Parameters of Slavery, a group of practitioners, including Aidan McQuade, the Director of Anti-Slavery International, and Kevin Bales, of Free the Slaves; experts in the history and legal history of enslavement, including Seymour Drescher, Paul Finkelman, Orlando Patterson, Rebecca Scott; and academic property lawyers, including Antony Honoré and James Penner. Funded by the United Kingdom's Arts and Humanities Research Council, this Research Network on the Legal Parameters of Slavery developed the 2012 *Bellagio-Harvard Guidelines on the Legal Parameters of Slavery*.

What emerged from our first meeting at the Rockefeller Foundation Bellagio Center was that, it was apparent that property lawyers and those individuals studying slavery, both contemporary and historical, had never truly engaged with each other as to the very nature of slavery. Antony Honoré, though not in attendance in Italy, loomed large in our conversations as he, nearly fifty years previously, had written an article which is now seen as part of the canon of property law entitled "Ownership", in which he set out the various incidents of ownership – those "powers attaching to the right of ownership".[33] In that study, Honoré explained that ownership was built on the substructure of possession: only when one possess a thing could he or she then use, manage,

---

31 See Jean Allain, *The Slavery Conventions: The Travaux Préparatoires of the 1926 League of Nations Convention and the 1956 United Nations Convention*, Martinus Nijhoff, 2008, pp. 495–498.

32 See United Nations Economic and Social Council, Slavery, the Slave Trade, and other forms of Servitude (Report of the Secretary-General), UN Doc. E/2357, 27 January 1953, p. 27 as reproduced in Jean Allain, *The Slavery Conventions: The Travaux Préparatoires of the 1926 League of Nations Convention and the 1956 United Nations Convention*, Martinus Nijhoff, 2008, p. 496.

33 Antony Honoré, "Ownership" in AG Guest (ed), *Oxford Essays in Jurisprudence*, 1961, p. 113.

profit, transfer or dispose of it. For Honoré and for property lawyers more generally (both within the common and civil law tradition), *possession is about control*. That was, to the ears of experts of slavery a revelation, as for them, enslavement was itself about the loss of agency, that diminution of autonomy which results from control being taken by another. In other words: *slavery is about control*.

With this as our fundamental understanding, we unpacked the exercise of those powers attaching to the right of ownership in the context of enslavement through Guidelines 2 of the *Bellagio-Harvard Guidelines*, which reads:

> In cases of slavery, the exercise of "the powers attaching to the right of ownership" should be understood as constituting control over a person in such a way as to significantly deprive that person of his or her individual liberty, with the intent of exploitation through the use, management, profit, transfer or disposal of that person. Usually this exercise will be supported by and obtained through means such as violent force, deception and/or coercion.

Let me here pause for a moment to relate a story about that understanding.

> In January 2013, I was invited to give evidence before the Joint Committee of the House of Commons and House of Lords at the British Parliament at Westminster. There I advocated including within what would become the 2015 *Modern Slavery Act*, the definition of slavery as set out in the 1926 League of Nations Convention.
>
> To this, Baroness Butler-Sloss, formerly a Lord Justice of Appeal, said to me: "why are you insisting on that old definition". Instead she made reference to Guideline 2 of the *Bellagio-Harvard Guidelines* and said "why don't you go directly to that, as people would understand it" as the "right of ownership seems too archine".
>
> And so I found myself in the awkward position of having argued for inclusion in law of a League of Nations definition, when the main legal voice on the Committee was pushing me to include the work I had helped develop into law. Well despite my best efforts, our interpretation of the definition of slavery did make it into the Bill drafted by that Joint Committee, only to be removed later in the legislative process in favour of a reference to the jurisprudence of the European Court of Human Rights.[34]

In line with the property law paradigm, which is at the heart of the 1926 definition of slavery, we made plain in the *Guidelines* that where enslavement

---

34 See Part 1(1), House of Lords, House of Commons – Joint Committee on the Draft Modern Slavery Bill, *Report Draft Modern Slavery Bill*, 8 April 2014 at www.publications.parliament.uk/pa/jt201314/jtselect/jtslavery/166/166.pdf.

was concerned, "ownership implies a background relationship of control", and that this control, in property law, is known as possession.

Let me digress once more, this time to consider this control/possession nexus which is fundamental to unpacking the potential of the internationally recognised definition of slavery. In so doing, it will also allow us to better understand the notion of *de facto* slavery.

> Let us consider a dispute between drug dealers – over a kilo of heroin. Unable to settle our differences, our feeble-minded dealers take their claim to court. First, the judge would say that in law, neither claimants can own the kilo of heroin, as it is illegal to do so. However, the judge will come to say that one of our dealers controls the heroin and thus possesses it – the result being *de facto* ownership – and sentence accordingly.
>
> Let us now shift our thoughts to apply this scenario to enslavement. Two people disputing the ownership of a person. These dimwits turn to a court of law, wherein the judge will determine that such ownership is illegal, but that one of the parties, having established control tantamount to possession, is guilty of enslavement.

Here then is the means of establishing slavery in a contemporary context, that it is about control – that one person controls another person *as if* they owned; that is: that they have established control tantamount to possession. Once that control is established, they can then exercise those other powers attaching to the right of ownership. As we say in the *Guidelines*: that control tantamount to possession "creates the factual conditions for the exercise of any or all of the other powers attaching to the right of ownership".[35]

Let me provide an example of what constitutes another power attaching to the right of ownership which meets the threshold of slavery when there is manifest control tantamount to possession: that of the buying or selling of a person. I often use the example of a football player who is "bought" and "sold" by clubs. First, we would recognise that such instances do not constitute slavery, as the control tantamount to possession is absent. The footballer can walk away, he need not go to another club, another city. More would be required: there would need to be evidence of control tantamount to possession – the type of control which we might term *dominion* over another. The type of control which people fundamentally rebel against, a type of control which more often than not is established through violence, as a

---

[35] See Guideline 3 – Possession is Foundational to Slavery, *Bellagio-Harvard Guidelines on the Legal Parameters of Slavery*, as found in Jean Allain, *The Legal Understanding of Slavery: From the Historical to the Contemporary*, (Oxford: Oxford University Press, 2012), pp. 375–380; and available in Arabic, French, Mandarin, Spanish, and Russian at: http://go.qub.ac.uk/bellagio-harvard.

means of subjugation. And so, the so-called buying or selling of a person, will only provide evidence of slavery,
The *Guidelines* therefore speak to the issue of buying or selling in the following manner:

> Buying, selling or otherwise transferring a person may provide evidence of slavery. Having established control tantamount to possession; the act of buying, selling or transferring that person will be an act of slavery.

The *Guidelines* follow this same template in speaking to using a person, profiting from a person, inheriting a person, or disposing, mistreating or neglecting a person. Likewise, *Guideline 4(c)* speaks of managing the use of a person in the following terms:

> Managing the use of a person may provide evidence of slavery. Having established control tantamount to possession; the act of managing that person will be an act of slavery.
> Evidence of such management of the use of a person may include direct management such as a brothel owner delegating power to a day manager in a situation of slavery in the context of sex work.

Conclusion

While Theo van Boven remains a beacon for those of us who seek to engage in international human rights law both as scholars and practitioners, the lesson I have brought with me this evening is that the role of legal scholar must be steeped in the history and the historical evolution of the normative content of the provisions with which we seek to engage.
It is only with this authority can one debunk myths – here related to universal jurisdiction to suppress the slave trade; tropes: of a *jus cogens* norm attached to forced labour; and of historical amnesia which has failed to recognise and provide guidance with regard to the normative content of servitude as being specific to what is probably the largest subset person being exploited: through debt bondage.
While these challenges to the *status quo* provide both clarity and coherence to the regime of human exploitation and the derivatives to be gained in international human rights law, it is becoming evident that the work which Aidan, I and others have undertaken, manifest in the 2012 *Bellagio-Harvard Guidelines*, not only bring the suppression of enslavement into the orbit of the law for the first time, but by capturing the lived experience of those who are enslaved today, they set the foundation for any scholarly examination, NGO intervention, or policy determination touching on human trafficking or contemporary forms of slavery.

This is no mean feat – the European Court of Human Rights considers that the prohibition against slavery, along with the prohibition against torture and the right to life enshrine "the basic values of the democratic societies making up the Council of Europe". Where previously that internationally recognised fundamental human right was deemed to be dead-letter law, as only applicable to legal-ownership of the past, the work of the human rights scholar, through archival research and legal analysis has paid divides: the law now recognises contemporary forms of slavery.

The Politics of Human Rights: Slavery and the Sustainable Development Goals

Aidan McQuade

First of all many thanks for having me. It is a great honour and pleasure to be here. Though it is regrettable that we meet here at the end of a year which I fear must be judged one of Europe's most disgraceful in recent memory.

2015 has been marked first by carnage off our Southern shores brought about in no small part by the failure of European leaders to establish safe migration routes for refugees, and by the slaughter on the streets of Paris, by fellow Europeans inspired by the slave states of Islamic State and Saudi Arabia, from whose atrocities so many refugees are fleeing.

More hopefully, this is also the year that the United Nations adopted the Sustainable Development Goals, which may be regarded as an effort of will to express the best of our human ideals in a year when much of the most craven of human behaviour has been on display.

The Sustainable Development Goals represent a considerable progression on the Millennium Development Goals that preceded them in that they are both more comprehensive and more rooted in a rights based approach.

The absence of fundamental rights related issues, such as slavery eradication, ending of caste based *apartheid* or advancement of the rule of law, meant that the Millennium Development Goals conveyed the impression that the ending of poverty was merely a technical challenge that required, in the main, the transfer of things to people who did not have things.

But the ending of poverty is also a political issue. Because often the reason that people don't have things is that they are excluded from the processes of development by more powerful actors. This is most clearly seen when considering the issue of slavery. Those who are enslaved are drawn from communities which are systematically excluded from power to enable their control by those who are more privileged. They include Dalits and Adivasi in South Asia, migrants in Europe, the Middle East, the Americas, South East Asia and West Africa, and women and children everywhere.

Prejudice and discrimination against certain groups on arbitrary bases such as caste, ethnicity, gender and religion is still frequently used as a basis upon which the more powerful exclude the more vulnerable from the processes of development. By doing so those same mechanisms of social exclusion also render those discriminated against more vulnerable to slavery.

There has been no progress worth noting on the eradication of slavery during the life of the Millennium Development Goals, a fact that is highlighted by the number 5.5 million. 5.5 million is the ILO's most recent estimate, made in

2012, of the number of children in slavery. It is the same as the ILO's estimate of the number of children in slavery in 2005.

In other words, in spite of all the other progress on poverty reduction and development, including a huge fall in the overall numbers of child labourers, during the period of the Millennium Development Goals, international development has completely passed by the millions of children and, for that matter, the tens of millions more adults in slavery across the world.

It is rare these days to come across anybody who explicitly supports slavery. Certainly there are those perpetrators who would like you to believe that they are doing their victims a favour. But by and large the political and business elites of the world are united in their condemnation of slavery, and will uniformly express anguish at the thought of children and vulnerable workers being subject to the cruelties of traffickers.

However that apparent consensus masks a more complex reality, in which the powerful remain wedded to systems of law and policy that facilitate the enslavement of poor and socially excluded workers.

For example many of you will be familiar with the reports of systematic use of forced labour of South Asian migrant workers in Qatar to build the infrastructure for the 2022 World Cup. Or you may have heard of the routine enslavement of domestic workers in Saudi Arabia. One distressing report by the BBC on 12 November 2015 related to an Indian domestic worker there who described her arm chopped off by her employer as a punishment. It should be noted that the Saudi authorities dispute her account, saying she lost her arm "trying to escape", and in denying complicity in mutilation they confirm complicity in slavery.

At the root of both these systems of enslavement is what is called the *Kafala* system, which is a "sponsorship" system that ties migrant workers to their employers to such an extent that even in the most abusive employment relationships, up to and including forced labour, the workers cannot change jobs or even leave the country to go home.

It is a cynical system to legally facilitate medieval levels of exploitation up to and including slavery across the entire Arabian peninsula.

It is also essentially the same system that the UK government has in place for overseas domestic workers which uses visas that tie workers to employers to such an extent that it *de facto* legalises trafficking for forced domestic servitude.

The cases of UK overseas domestic worker visas, and Arabian *Kafala* show how too frequently the law, intentionally or otherwise, can be a means to facilitate enslavement.

In other parts of the world decent anti-slavery law is made a mockery of because the rule of law simply does not pertain in a jurisdiction. For example in India corrupt police forces and overburdened court systems mean that legal protections from slavery are meaningless for those most vulnerable to slavery, namely those socially excluded groups, such as Dalits, Adavasi, and Muslims.

We saw this in the course of a piece of research that we did into forced and child labour in Indian garment manufacture. In this we spoke to children, many of them Muslims, who worked in some of the garment workshops of Delhi. They told us that the only encounters they had with the police were when they were arrested and held as hostages to stop work because their employers had not paid the appropriate bribes.

In India there is also such limited labour inspection that it will never trouble those factory owners who enslave young women and girls, many of them Dalits, to produce the cotton thread that doubtless forms a sizeable percentage of the garments we are each wearing this evening.

Just to give one illustration of what that means in human terms: in the course of that research into trafficking in Indian garment manufacture, Anti-Slavery spoke to the mother of one young 20 year old woman who worked in a cotton spinning mill there. She described visiting her daughter:

I spoke to her in a room provided for visitors, she said, because visitors are not allowed to go inside the mill or hostel. My daughter told me that she was suffering with fever and vomiting often. ... I met with the manager and requested him to give leave to my daughter because she was unwell. I told him that I would send my daughter back once she was better. But the manager refused saying that there was a shortage of workers therefore they cannot grant leave. He also assured me that they would take care of my daughter and asked me not to worry.

A week later she received a message to say now she could collect her daughter. She was dead.

If abuses such as this are brought to light there is no sanction: Europe does not exclude from our markets slavery produced goods and business executives who knowingly profit from the uses of forced labour in their supply chains are not held criminally liable. Hence slavery tainted supply chains continue to ensnare us, from the cotton we wear, to the coltan in our mobile, to the food we eat.

So: when we consider the contemporary manifestations of slavery and child labour across the world we see that slavery emerges in the opportunities for exploitation that are presented to unscrupulous individuals in national and international law and policy as it relates in particular to education and human development, employment, trade, migration and rule of law itself. And the persistence of these systems long after their exposure shows how the powerful vested interests that benefit from these systems ensure their maintenance.

Slavery can only really thrive where governments fail in their duties of promoting human development and protecting human rights.

Currently in India Prime Minister Modi proposes to reduce factory inspections, and permit child labour as a means of reinforcing the caste system, amongst other so-called labour market reforms. Whatever Modi's other intentions are with these changes, the consequence will be to make forced and child labour abuses much more likely across India and hence increase the likelihood that any goods or commodities produced there are tainted by slavery-like practices.

A few weeks ago I was visiting cocoa-growing communities in Ghana. There the risk of child labour is exacerbated by the fact that too few of those communities have schools, and even if the kids get to school there is so little provision of vocational and entrepreneurial education for adolescents and young adults that many of them become vulnerable to trafficking for forced labour once they leave school, as they follow risky paths in search of scarce decent work.

We see this again and again, that the majority of the underlying causes of slavery, such as state-acquiescence in caste-based discrimination, the toleration of child marriage, undermining of the rule of national and international law, the failure to establish safe migration routes for vulnerable workers seeking decent work, or the decriminalised international trade in slavery produced goods and services are profoundly political.

The Scottish comedian Billy Connolly once said, "Hypocrisy is the Vaseline of political intercourse".

We see this with the current UK government claims that it wishes to be a world leader in the struggle against slavery. And yet just this month Sir Simon McDonald, Permanent Secretary at the Foreign Office, said that human rights are no longer a priority in the Foreign Office, and instead was supplanted by the "prosperity" agenda. That leads to their warm embrace of Prime Minister Modi and the prospect of trade deals with an India whose supply chains are rife with forced and child labour, and, even more bizarrely, with Saudi Arabia, who remain valued partners in spite of their systematic and entrenched practices of slavery, their intent to crucify a child for protesting for democracy, and their creation and sponsorship of DAESH, Islamic State.

We see this hypocrisy also in relation to the poisonous immigration debate across Europe. We have seen how establishing safe migration for vulnerable workers is a key issue in ending trafficking. I have already described how both the Arabian *Kafala* system and the UK's systems of tied visas offer opportunities of legal migration to poor working people that are little more than supply channels for the provision of forced labour to traffickers.

But the discussions on safe international migration remain mired in xenophobic cant, which both confuses and is confused by the political discourse on trafficking.

At the height of the refugee crisis in the Mediterranean this summer, we heard the insistent descriptions by European politicians of those who were facilitating transport of refugees across the Mediterranean as "traffickers". Trafficking, by definition, is the movement of people for the purposes of forced labour or sexual exploitation. It was very clear, very quickly from diligent reporters on the ground in the Mediterranean that what was going on was not trafficking but the facilitation of smuggling. It is true that once these refugees get to Europe that they will be highly vulnerable to traffickers, and seeing that

The Politics of Human Rights: Slavery and the Sustainable Development Goals

some of the smugglers may expand their operations into trafficking. But this is at least as much because of the failure of Europe's leaderships to establish safe and legal migration routes, as it is anything to do with the smugglers.

But politicians try to disguise their inaction in the face of the moral imperative of this refugee crisis by the conflation of smuggling and trafficking. By obfuscating the issues they seek to buy political breathing space in the face of the mounting carnage. When faced with the horrors of the Mediterranean this summer, it was easier for politicians to make grand statements blaming migrant deaths on evil traffickers, rather than doing their jobs by seeking the causes of the crisis and identifying more effective responses.

So given this scale of challenge, and the shape of human history in which we find ourselves, for there to be any progress towards our better ideals, as represented by the Sustainable Development Goals, in particular the targets relating to forced and child labour, we, as a human community, must do much better that we, as a European community have managed this year.

So this is where it gets difficult. Because fundamental to making progress on this issue we will have to confront the powerful vested interests who benefit from the way the world currently is.

For example if the international community is serious in its efforts against slavery how can we continue to acquiesce in the ready access to international markets and warm inclusion to the international polity of Uzbekistan, Saudi Arabia and Qatar, to name but three states, which, with differing degrees of cynicism, have effectively legalised slavery within their borders.

Or, as I mentioned, in spite of its recent casting of itself as a global leader against slavery it is unlikely that the UK has for a moment considered the potential impact that its naked disdain for the European Court of Human Rights will have on the rule of international law in general and as it relates to slavery in particular: that Court has been vital since 2000 in forcing governments across Europe, including the UK, to properly respect the rights of victims of slavery. Any credible international struggle against slavery must therefore confront the British government on this, one of their most cherished political prejudices.

And, another political issue: should India be made a permanent member of the UN Security Council while its toleration of caste-based violence is so high, and its efforts to end slavery are so paltry?

To end slavery, as the Sustainable Development Goals propose, would be a considerable advance both in the struggles to advance human rights and to end poverty. But it demands a recognition that tackling slavery is a fundamental political and development issue. However, until now, development and humanitarian policy-makers and practitioners have barely even been aware of these issues and so have failed to address them in any systematic way

Frequently, such as in the brick kilns and quarries of South Asia, or the agricultural sector of West Africa, slavery and child labour are openly practiced. Therefore there should be a requirement of every credible development and humanitarian agency to consider if they could contribute

towards the reduction of slavery and child labour within every community with which they work. This may not always be possible. But asking the question, and considering carefully the dynamics of power and discrimination could lead to empowerment of some who would previously have been overlooked.
There should also be much more conscious focus by development and humanitarian policy makers and practitioners on diminishing the vulnerability to slavery of those communities. For example, ensuring that the children, particularly the daughters, of brick kiln workers and manual scavengers in South Asia, or cocoa farmers in West Africa have access to proper education, could help break the transmission of slavery and poverty across generations. And ensuring that the curriculum promotes human rights, in particular those of girls, and toleration for all would help erode the prejudices that permit human beings to enslave and exploit others.
National governments and the international donor community must as a priority establish funding models to ensure this. In the face of the medievalism of Boko Haram, Islamic State and Saudi Arabia this challenge becomes more urgent by the day.
Beyond the development and humanitarian sectors the issue of slavery must become a centrepiece of diplomacy, trade and migration policy. In particular there is a need for a clear recognition of the brutal reality that tied visas are *de facto* licences for trafficking across the world. And governments who truly wish to be regarded as world leaders in the struggle against slavery must refuse to turn blind eyes to the systematic failures in national and international rule of law and policy that facilitates slavery across the globe.
It is a hard lesson of history that when the moral courage of political leaders fails in the face of prejudice and vested interests it is the vulnerable who are usually the ones to pay in the bloody routine of violence that ensues. We can see that in the carnage off our Southern shores. We can see that in the brutal practices of slavery that we as a human society continue to permit across the world.

200 years ago people like Equiano and Clarkson in Europe, and in the Americas, Sam Sharpe, Nat Turner, Touissant, the Maroons decided, for diverse reasons, to try to end slavery, so morally repugnant did they find it. In doing so they took on a system that the writer Adam Hochschild has compared in the equivalence of its power to the oil industry today. In ending the slave trade through force of arms and force of argument in a mere 20 years they showed what could be achieved when there is the collective will and the audacity of ambition to do so.

Clarkson, Equiano, Turner and Sharpe, the Maroons, the Quakers, and the nascent trades unions have been substantially written out of the history of that struggle, first by Wilberforce's sons, and largely forgotten subsequently. That historiographical injustice contributes not just to the misremembering of what happened, but the misunderstanding of why it happened. The achievements of 200 years ago were a classic example, in Bobby Kennedy's phrase, of numberless diverse acts of courage and belief shaping the history of the time.

Whatever our differences, one thing that unites us is that we are all citizens in this world. And that brings with it not just rights but responsibilities. We have the responsibility to remember properly. We have the responsibility to think and to understand. We have the responsibility to act, to "Do to others what you want them to do to you." And we have the responsibility to remember that when we act with common purpose, in spite of all our flaws and diverse motives, that still, together, we can overcome.

Also published in the Theo van Boven Lecture Series:

Theo van Boven, From Exclusion to Inclusion, 2011,
ISBN 978-94-000-0179-4 (Volume 1)

Carlos Villán Durán, The Emerging Right to Peace: Its Legal Foundations, 2014, ISBN 978-1-78068-237-2 (Volume 2)

www.ingramcontent.com/pod-product-compliance
Ingram Content Group UK Ltd.
Pitfield, Milton Keynes, MK11 3LW, UK
UKHW051848210426
5322IPUK00024B/607